Murder and Mishap

Sudden Death in Victorian Sheffield

By Shirley Baxter

Illustrated by Jane Horton

Sheffield General Cemetery Trust

Acknowledgements

The Sheffield General Cemetery Trust (SGCT) grew out of the Friends of the Sheffield General Cemetery group which was formed in 1989. Over the years many volunteers have diligently researched and recorded the lives of people buried and commemorated in the Cemetery. The work of all those volunteers contributes to the records kept by SGCT which form the basis of this book. Shirley Baxter is one of the latest in that long line of volunteers and has compiled and written this latest book for the SGCT.

Special thanks are due to Jane Horton for her drawings and to Andrew Littlewood for the photographs of the graves. Alex Quant assisted in the production of this book which was edited by Laura Alston and Jo Meredith.

The SGCT is grateful for information about Robert Fossett and Fossett's Circus supplied by descendants A .and G. Williams.

Thanks also to Sheffield City Council and the National Heritage Lottery Fund 'Parks for People' Project for supporting the production of the book.

Printed by Mensa Printers 323 Abbeydale Road Sheffield S7 1FS

ISBN 978-0-9539-9945-3

*"Stop passenger and read this stone
and think of how quickly I was gone.
Death does not always warnings give,
therefore be careful how you live."*

Memorial inscription for Samuel Warburton
who is buried in Sheffield General Cemetery
(Anglican plot C2 93)

CONTENTS

INTRODUCTION

The General Cemetery was proudly advertised in the Sheffield Independent, 10 September 1836, as a "beautiful place of Sepulture, whose Picturesque and Architectural attractions are well known to the Inhabitants of this Town...Vaults of almost every description and size, and finished in the most complete manner, may, by early Application, be Purchased upon reasonable Terms; and Graves, in various situations, the most open or the most secluded, are also disposable to the choice of the Public". Today the Cemetery functions as a popular green, open space and a haven for wildlife. A designated Conservation Area, it has Grade II* status on the National Register of Historic Parks and Gardens.

By 1978, the year of the last burial, the Cemetery held 87,000 people. While many of the residents lived unremarkable lives, and died unknown to all but their families and friends, others were suddenly and unexpectedly struck down and, as a result, their deaths, requiring an inquest, were reported in the local newspapers. These reports might then be syndicated to local papers in other places, depending on the amount of interest (or perhaps, shortage of news!). It is these newspaper reports, along with the burial records, memorial inscriptions and other information held by the Sheffield General Cemetery Trust, which have provided much of the information on which the accounts in this book are based.

In the nineteenth century, long before the days of health and safety regulations, risk assessments and accountability, accidents were frequent. Open fires in homes, inadequate or non-existent protection in the work environment and the use of horses on the roads, meant that often someone who was alive one day, was gone the next. Modern medicine was still in its infancy and for most of the nineteenth century, there was little that could be done for complex injuries other than to offer comfort and possibly pain relief – and not always that.

To some extent social class was a pointer to the type of accident. For example, it was the middle classes, able to afford horses and carriages, who suffered most from trap and riding accidents, and the poorer, working classes who died from accidents at work or burns incidents in the home. As is well known, grinders were frequently injured or killed by the grinding wheels on which they worked, while those working on steel manufacture were at risk of molten metal spilling. There was no personal protection equipment, and no engagement with the concept of employers or owners being responsible for the safety of those on their premises. Children drowned in unfenced or poorly fenced dam ponds, which often lacked warning signs. Of those who died because of the Dale Dyke Dam collapse, most were working class people, living near to their places of work in homes built on flood plains. Adventurous youth, then as now, could be led into danger on impulse, and the ready availability of laudanum, a tincture of opium used to suppress pain or coughs, provided opportunities for accidental overdose.

Life was unpredictable. John Gunsen, the engineer who was responsible for the building of Dale Dyke Dam, narrowly escaped death when the dam he was inspecting suddenly gave way, and David Davy, founder of Davy Brothers, Engineers, Wheelwrights and Iron Founders, was killed in his factory by a fan installed with a design fault.

Inquests were generally held in the most conveniently situated public house. The more sensational the death, or the more prominent the victim, the more likely it was that sensationalist accounts would be published in the local papers in detail. A shocking murder could be revisited several times, feeding the readers' interest with often graphic detail. Witness evidence was reported in full, even if this meant repetition of information.

As the century progressed, and new modes of mechanical transport were introduced, the unwary, still not accustomed to the dangers of mechanical means of transport, could easily meet with fatal accidents, particularly when horse drawn vehicles fell foul of traction engines, as in the Froggatt Edge Accident, described in the Trust's earlier book "Danger and Despair". Trains, with unfenced railway lines, were responsible for many fatal accidents. Some people tripped on the line, some walking alongside the tracks were struck glancing blows, and of course, some used the train as a mode of suicide. With the arrival of the twentieth century, trams and cars increasingly played a part in accidental deaths.

The stories in this book are the product of thirty years of research by volunteers, and we hope they will add to your enjoyment of this beautiful and historical site. One of the joys of researching residents of the cemetery is the glimpse it gives us into the past. Just for a moment, something of their lives and times is revealed, occasionally vibrantly.

Note – Not all the graves are accessible, and many monuments in the Anglican section were cleared by Sheffield City Council in 1979/80 when the site's restoration began from its then derelict state into the attractive Cemetery park that we enjoy today.

DEATH ON THE ROAD

Marriot Hall

Marriot Hall, who died in a riding accident, was well connected. He was also the uncle of Sir Arthur Hall, who developed Sheffield Medical School, and of T. Walter Hall, one of the founders of The Hunter Archaeological Society. A doctor, he was married to Sarah Bingham Taylor Firth, the daughter of Mark Firth. The Sheffield and Rotherham Independent 18 March 1878 reported that:

'Mr Marriot came from a Sheffield family; Mr John Hall, surgeon, Victoria street, being his brother, and Mr John Hall, Norbury, and Mr Marriott Hall, Kiveton Park, his cousins. He commenced his medical career as assistant house surgeon at the Infirmary. He was subsequently the house surgeon there…and [later] he was for a time in practice with his brother. Subsequently he conducted his practice alone…Mr Hall was of the courteous, genial, gentlemanly school of medical men, whose presence in the sick room does almost more good than the remedies they apply…A warm hearted friend, a rare companion, a skilful surgeon, and a genial and cheerful guide has passed away'.

On the day he was tragically killed, Mr Hall had planned to visit those patients on his list who lived a distance from town, and so was riding 'one of his horses, a high spirited animal rendered more so because of having been kept a good deal in the stables'. Returning from his first visit by way of Ranmoor Road on his way to Broomhall Park, he turned into Endcliffe Vale Road. The horse began to get restive and very soon uncontrollable, rearing and swerving. Mr Hall kept his seat, struggling to regain control. Efforts from a passer-by to help failed. The horse swerved to one side, stumbled, and fell on top of its rider.

11

The horse was apparently unhurt, but Mr Hall's head hit the kerb with great force. He was carried to the lodge of Mr Firth's house, Oakbrook, where he regained consciousness long enough to say to Mark Firth's coachman, who lived there, " I am afraid, Outram, I am badly hurt." Adding, "Oh, my poor head." After this he lost consciousness again and died seven hours later.

On the day of the funeral the blinds were drawn in the houses of Glossop Road and the surrounding streets, and tradesmen closed their shops. Although there was a large crowd, everyone was respectfully quiet and orderly as the cortege passed. Thousands of people remained in the cemetery after the service to view the grave. Mark Firth himself was so saddened by the death of his son in law that he was unable to attend.

Marriott Hall was 39 when he died. He is buried with his wife in Plot W1 145/146, next to the Firth monument.

Thomas Mahonie

Thomas Mahonie was a successful dental surgeon. He was killed in a carriage accident in October 1886. Mr Mahonie had planned to take the train to Deepcar to attend to a patient. He was being driven to the station in a low four wheeled phaeton by his coachman, Edward Rushworth. Also in the carriage was his son Evelyn. Unfortunately, the shafts of the carriage were rather short for the horse, and feeling the carriage touching its hind quarters, it began to kick and plunge before suddenly hurtling ahead uncontrollably. Mr Mahonie and his son pulled on the brake, but the horse kept going to Church Street, where there were several stationary vehicles whose owners were at a meeting in Cutlers' Hall. Witnesses said that they saw Mr Mahonie stand up and clutch the coachman. At this moment, an omnibus was seen coming towards them, and Mr Mahonie leapt from the carriage opposite Cutlers' Hall. He fell heavily on his back, possibly because

of catching his arm on the wheel guard. Almost immediately after this, bystanders succeeded in stopping the horse, although the carriage hit the omnibus and the son and coachman were thrown out. They were not injured but Mr Mahonie had fractured his skull and, despite all assistance, died in the late afternoon.

Two years previously he had suffered an accident mounting his horse, and still walked with a limp, but he had always enjoyed riding and driving a carriage. Mrs Mahonie was doubly bereaved when nine years later her eldest son Evelyn, also a surgeon dentist, died aged 28. Her other son, Norman, died in Madras in 1901. Mrs Mahonie died in 1915.

Thomas Mahonie is buried in the cleared Anglican area of the Cemetery, in plot U1 160, with his wife, Evelyn and a son who died in infancy.

Mary Cockayne

Reporting the accident which killed Mary Cockayne, the Independent 3 March 1887 commented 'Vehicular mishaps in Sheffield through horses taking fright are of common occurrence, but it seldom happens that we have to record a serious, and unfortunately, fatal trap accident as that which occurred about four miles from the town yesterday afternoon'.

Miss Cockayne was a friend of Miss Florence Witty, the daughter of the Rev J F Witty, who had the use of her father's low, light trap for the afternoon. For the first part of the drive Miss Witty was accompanied by another friend, Miss Suckley, but shortly afterwards Miss Suckley got down and her place was taken by Miss Cockayne, the daughter of a chemist who had died a few months previously. They drove out to Hollow Meadows, before turning to come back. As they reached the Norfolk Arms, the horse stumbled. Miss Witty, who was driving, realised that there was something wrong with the harness and a moment later the bridle, bluffs and bit came off and hung down between the horse's legs. The horse immediately took fright and bolted. Miss Witty could not check it and Miss Cockayne said she was going to jump out of the trap. Miss Witty, although frightened herself, thought this was too dangerous, and advised her to hold on tight. Just as the horse seemed to be slowing slightly, they met an open carriage coming towards them. The horse, unnerved, speeded up again, swerved into the ditch at the side of the road and Miss Witty was thrown out. Miss Cockayne, terrified, was hurtled past two more carriages. She cried out for help, but no one could do anything. One witness saw her standing up and thought perhaps she was preparing to jump. Another witness saw her jump but, unfortunately, she did not jump clear, her clothes were caught in the trap, and she was dragged along for a short distance. She was carried to the Post Office at Rivelin Bridge and although medical help arrived quickly, Miss Cockayne died soon afterwards from head injuries. Miss Witty was shocked and bruised but otherwise unhurt.

Mary Cockayne's mother, having lost her husband and only daughter within months of each other, later went to live with her son, a Church of England clergyman, and his family, in Chichester. They were still all together in 1911.

Mary is buried with her father in plot T1 73, in the cleared Anglican area.

William Moorhouse

A 'Shocking Fatality near Baslow' was reported in the Sheffield and Rotherham Independent 7 June 1892. It was Whitsun, and Baslow was crowded with holiday makers. Coaches, wagonettes, and other vehicles were following each other in quick succession. William Moorhouse, a postman who lived in Monmouth Street was making the most of a day's holiday. A keen 'bicyclist' he planned to ride to Baslow accompanying his sweetheart, a servant in the house of a Mrs Wightman in Broomgrove Road who would be a passenger in a waggonette.

'1903 Daimler 22 wagonette', Blue Mountains Local Studies (Australia, 1910)

'They both started in good spirits…..Moorhouse on his bicycle was able to keep company with the wagonette, occasionally exchanging conversation with her and with other passengers, and at other times riding on either before or behind……….All went well till Baslow was reached, but as the wagonette was passing the church, Moorhouse rode up on the near side between the wagonette and the causeway. Whether he was intending to pass on in front or not is not clear, but the road space available was very narrow… At that point the pathway is protected at the edge by an occasional projecting stone, and it appears that the treadle of Moorhouse's bicycle caught one of these stones. Instantly his wheel was forced round – for he was going at a rapid pace – and the poor fellow was thrown to the ground. He fell immediately in front of the fore wheel, and before the driver could pull up, both wheels of the vehicle had passed over him.'

Death was almost instantaneous; his head and body being crushed. The wagonette carried nearly 30 passengers and was estimated to weigh not less than 50 cwts. There was nothing anyone could do, except to look after his very distressed sweetheart. William was described as 'a quiet, steady, and respectable young fellow' who 'bore a good character' at the post office.

William was buried alone in the cleared Anglican area in plot Z1 88.

Charles Robert Partington

One of the most dramatic memorials in Sheffield General Cemetery was that erected in 1903 by Lt Colonel Bingham and the Veterans' Association to the memory of Charles Robert Partington, secretary of the Association and formerly sergeant of the 1st Royal Dragoons. A stone replica of his helmet rested on top of a roughhewn stone, and against each side leaned a bronze carbine and sword. A plaque beneath the helmet explained that ' he charged with General Scarlett's Brigade at Balaclava, twice cutting through the Russians, on October 25th, 1854 and was the same day severely wounded while covering the retirement from the Charge of the Light brigade'. The monument no longer exists in its original form. The bronze carbine and sword, and the plaque, were stolen long ago. Later the stone helmet was also taken but rediscovered in 2003.

At the time he enlisted, Charles was only 17, having run away from his boarding school the year before with two friends to enlist (extract from letter from grandson, J R Partington.). According to newspaper accounts, Charles also fought at the siege of Sevastopol (1854-5).

It is not known when Charles left the army but he was a civilian by the time of his marriage to Emily Methley of Rotherham in 1866, and for many years he was employed by the timber merchants, Messrs Sale and Feather. As secretary of Sheffield Crimean and Indian Veterans Association he 'gave freely…of his ability and his time …to assist old soldiers in distressed circumstances'. He was described as a 'true, noble hearted and generous man who had loved his fellow men.' (Sheffield Independent March 18, 1902)

Ironically, having survived great danger in his youth, Charles was killed, as the inscription acidly explained, 'through his horse falling twice upon badly kept slippery granite on Attercliffe Road.' He was thrown from his trap and died in the Royal Hospital following severe head injuries.

He was buried with full military honours. According to the newspaper account, the procession was led by a detachment of mounted police, followed by a 12-man firing party, then the band, with drums draped in black, playing the funeral march. The coffin, covered by a Union Jack, with his helmet resting on top, was carried on a gun carriage drawn by 6 horses. Hundreds of people lined the streets to watch.

Charles Partington is buried in plot B1 18 in the Anglican area.

Alfred Holmes

Alfred Holmes was a measure and rules manufacturer, of the firm Tyzack and Holmes. He lived at Hodsock Park, Worksop, with his wife and Percy Tyzack and four servants. Although he did not die until 2 June 1902, the accident which led to his death happened on March 29th of that year. He and his wife had been to a meet of Lord Galway's hounds in Sandbeck Park, and as they 'were leaving by the entrance of Maplas Hill, his horse shied. The shaft of the carriage caught in the ironwork of the gates and both Mr. and Mrs. Holmes were thrown out. Mrs. Holmes escaped with a few bruises, and a severe shaking, but her husband was not so fortunate. Mr. Holmes fell under the horse's body, and the animal's hoofs inflicted terrible injuries to his face and head.' (Sheffield Daily Telegraph 3 June 1902) Having survived the accident, it was hoped that he would eventually recover, but then there was a sudden relapse and he died.

The Telegraph article continued: 'Of a quiet and retiring disposition, Mr. Holmes took no active part in public affairs, but was well known in commercial circles in Sheffield, and he will be much missed by a large number of friends. A keen follower of the best forms of outdoor sport, he was the treasurer of the Wednesday Football Club, with which organisation he had been connected for many years. Mr. Holmes leaves a widow and two children.'

Alfred Holmes is buried in the family grave plot FF 1 in the Nonconformist area of the Cemetery.

Walter Ellis

Walter Ellis was a pocketknife and edge tool grinder. He and his wife Harriet had seven children. By the time of his death in 1909, he was 62, the secretary of the Edge Tool Grinders' Society and a well-known trade union official.

Mr Ellis was crossing Winter Street when he was knocked down by a tram car, on its way from Walkley to the city. He was taken to the Royal Hospital in the Fire Brigade ambulance but on arrival was found to have died from his head injuries.

'Sheffield Tramway tramcar 74 at the National Tramway Museum, Crich',
Photograph by Gregory Deryckère

Walter Ellis is buried with his wife in plot M1 87, in the cleared Anglican area.

John (Jack) Richardson

John Richardson, known as Jack, was 11 when he was knocked down and killed by a car in 1920. Cars were not as common as they are now; for many people, they were unaffordable. So Jack, walking along the road near Fox House with five friends, would be aware that there was occasional traffic, but not particularly alert, and he and his friends amused themselves by tossing a tennis ball across the road between them.

The Sheffield Independent reported what happened next:
"According to one [of the boys] George Oliver, of 39 Randall Street, they picked up the ball to allow a motor cycle to pass, and before they started playing again, a motor car, driven by Dr Wilkinson, of the Sheffield Royal Hospital, came along. One of the boys shouted a warning, but the victim of the accident, John Richardson, aged 11, of 109 Harwood Street, appeared not to hear, and the right-hand mudguard of the car caught him. He was knocked down and one of the wheels passed over his head."

Dr Wilkinson had been taking a trip into Derbyshire with friends before this horrific accident. Instead he found himself urgently driving back to the hospital, but the child was declared dead on arrival.

John Richardson is buried in the cleared Anglican section of the Cemetery, in plot N1 176, with his parents.

DEATH BY DROWNING

Sheffield Flood Victims

There are 77 flood victims buried in the Cemetery, the majority from the Neepsend area. Some are nameless, injured so badly by some of the formidable debris carried along by the flood that they were unrecognizable. The unidentified were buried at the expense of the Sheffield Union in public graves in the Cemetery, as were those who had no family who could afford to bury them, or no family left at all.

The shocking suddenness of the flood on the night of 12th March 1864 was the result of the catastrophic collapse of the new Dale Dyke or Bradfield dam, built by the Sheffield Water Company in response to the rapidly growing city's need for water. Villages, farms, bridges, public houses, and work premises were swept away as the water hurtled towards the city, bringing boulders, uprooted trees, bodies, building debris and broken machinery with it. The areas around Neepsend, Hillsborough and Owlerton were affected very badly; for days after the tragedy bodies were still being found during the endless mud clearing. The following seven stories are all about victims of the flood.

The Appleby family

The body of Mary Appleby, a widow, aged 62 years, was found in Jordan Meadows. She was the mother of John Cowton Appleby and grandmother of John's niece, Mary, aged 13, who also died in the flood. John was a grocer, from Hillsborough, and a widower, his wife Ellen having died the previous year. The census records for 1861 for

John Appleby are damaged and provide little information, but the entry for his mother, Mary Appleby, shows that she was earning her living as a seamstress, and that Mary aged 10, the daughter of Stephen Cowton Appleby, was living with her in Norwich Street. Stephen Cowton Appleby lived in Altrincham and Mary was the daughter of Stephen's first marriage. By 1864 he had remarried and had a young family. It looks as if Mary was brought up by her grandmother, following the death of her mother. When John's wife Ellen died, leaving a two-year-old daughter, Annie Maria, it seems probable that Mary went to live with John to look after her second motherless granddaughter, taking the young Mary with her. Annie Maria Appleby, three years old in 1864, was the only one of the family to survive.

After the disaster, Cowton Appleby, the younger brother of John, applied for letters of administration. He is described as a collector of rents and debts, and the uncle and guardian of Annie Maria Appleby, the only child of the deceased. Later, as the administrator of his mother's estate, he lodged a claim against the Water Company for lost property, including clothing, furniture, a small library of books, and burial expenses which he valued at £39 13s. He was awarded £24. For loss of stock and property belonging to his brother, he claimed £98 7s 4d and was awarded £65. For the welfare of his brother's child, he claimed £750 and was awarded £200. He also claimed £100 for the loss of his mother; that claim is listed as 'withdrawn.'

Stephen Cowton Appleby, the father of Mary, claimed £5 and was awarded 11s 6d.for loss of clothing, time spent in the search and for burial expenses. He claimed £200 for the loss of his daughter but was awarded £12 2s.

Annie Maria was brought up by her aunt, Elizabeth Swift, and her husband Charles. They had one daughter two years older than Annie, while Cowton Appleby already had two sons and went on to have several more. Unfortunately, nothing is known of Annie after 1871.

John Cowton Appleby, his mother Mary, and his niece Mary are buried in plot B3 175 in the cleared Anglican area. Buried with them is another brother, William Appleby, aged 22, silversmith.

William Bethel

William Bethel is listed in the burial record as being a cold steel roller aged 36 from Masborough. He was married and in 1861 had children aged 2 and three months.

William Bethel was employed by Messrs Barker and Johnson of the Limerick Wire and Rolling Mills and was the only man on duty at the Limerick Wheel on the night of the disaster. His body, disfigured and scalded, was found some time later, under debris in the workplace. It is not known whether he drowned or was killed by an explosion of the furnaces. The works premises were so badly damaged that the firm's losses, including the loss of manufactured goods and goods in the process of manufacture, was estimated by the surviving partner, Mr Johnson, at a cost of £12,000. (Mr Barker lodged at Malin Bridge and had also been swept away in the deluge.)

William's wife Elizabeth applied for letters of administration after his death. William left less than £50. In these sources he was described as a steel and metal roller and it is confirmed that he died at the Limerick Steel Mills on 12 March 1864.

Elizabeth remarried four years later. In the 1871 and 1881 census she was visiting other households, and is described as an 'accountant's wife', although her husband was not with her on either occasion. She was still alive in 1891, by now widowed again, living with her eldest daughter.

William Bethel is buried in plot X2 161, a public grave, in the cleared Anglican area.

The Gannon family

There are six people with the name of Gannon buried in a public grave in the Cemetery: John, 36, Sarah, 30, Henry, 11, Peter, 5, William, 4, and Margaret, 4 months. There is nothing in the burial records to suggest their relationships, but they are all from Neepsend Gardens. All the bodies were found in Neepsend on 12 March, except for John and Margaret, who were found on 13th March. The Sheffield Flood archive lists two more children John, 9, and Sarah Ann, 2, but they are not recorded in the Cemetery's burial records. Either their bodies were never found, or they are among the unidentified children buried in the Cemetery.

Peter and Henry were listed together as among the dead gathered at Sheffield Workhouse. It is probable that these Gannons are the family whose terrifying experience was described in the Sheffield Independent for 15 March 1864:

"Close to the river was a row of low white- washed cottages, the most eastern of which, standing a little way from the rest, was occupied by John Gannon, a labourer, his wife, and six children. The water rose to a considerable height in the bedrooms, and appalling were the cries for help and mercy of the inmates. The house was so full of water that he and his household climbed upon the roof, and there clung together with desperate tenacity. They had been there but a few minutes, when the house was swept away as if it had been pasteboard. A wild shriek was heard for a moment and they were plunged in the whirl of waters, and the entire family immediately perished."

The burial records do not give John Gannon's occupation, but there is a claim listed in the Sheffield Flood archive by John Brown, Marine Store Keeper, 'Creditor for Money paid to the West Yorkshire Loan Society.....for the said John Gannon or now payable' for £1 10s. It gives the address of John Gannon as Neills Buildings, Neepsend, and his job as 'Ostler and Gardener'.

The Gannons are buried in plot MM 42, a public grave in the Nonconformist area.

The Coggin (Coggan) family

The report in the Independent which featured the Gannon family also wrote:

"A labourer, named Coggan, and his wife, living a short distance beyond Gannon's, had gone to attend the funeral of a sister of one of them. They had left at home their three children, the eldest of whom was about ten years. The children slept in the same bed on the ground floor, and were drowned as they slept."

Three children with the surname of Coggin (but spelled Coggan in other sources) are buried in the Cemetery, their address given as Neepsend. They were Alfred, aged 13, Eliza, 8, and William, 6. They were the children of William and Elizabeth Coggan. William is described as a tanner in the 1851 and 1861 Census returns and probably worked at Mr Mill's Tannery opposite their home. The fate of another child, James, a few months old in 1861, is not known.

The Coggins are buried in plot G2 126, a public grave in the Anglican area.

Mrs Albert (Halbert)

Mrs Albert, of Neepsend Lane, the wife of a skinner who also worked at the same tannery, died with two of her children. Listed as Halbert, she is buried in the Cemetery but unless her children were among the unidentified, they are buried elsewhere.

Samuel Harrison, in his account of the Sheffield Flood, described what happened to this family. Thomas Albert had been awoken by the noise of the flood and seeing that the water was rising rapidly up the walls of the ground floor, alerted the family. He picked up his three-year-old son, while his wife clutched to the back of his shirt but before any other move could be made, the water burst in through the door. Mrs Albert was knocked down, her clutch so desperate that her husband's shirt was torn off his body. He waded through the water and left the little boy on some steps out of reach of the water. However, when he returned to help his wife and other children, he was himself knocked down by falling masonry, and was too late. They were drowned and the house largely destroyed.

Thomas Halbert later claimed £300 for the loss of his wife and children. He was awarded £50.

Mrs (H)Albert is buried in plot MM 25, a public grave, in the Nonconformist area.

The Peters family

Also buried in the Cemetery are the Peters children, Jane, 10, Julia, 4 and Christopher, 1 year 9 months. They are the children of Thomas, a skinner, and Jane Peters, and lived in Neepsend Lane. Their fate is described in the Sheffield Independent:

"In the next house to Albert, was Mrs. Peters and four children. Her husband was in Lincolnshire, and she was alone with the children. She escaped into a neighbour's house with one of the children, but the other three were drowned. Several of these houses were so low that the bedrooms were not a refuge, and the inmates had no alternative but to try to reach taller houses, where they could get beyond the reach of the water. "

Mrs Peters had escaped with the fourth child, Mary Alice, who was 4. Thomas Peters claimed £100 for the loss of his children. He was awarded £15. After the tragedy, the family moved south. By 1871 the Peters family were in Hitchin, Hertfordshire, with Alice, and ten years later in Southwark. They had three more children.

Thomas Peters claimed £100 for the loss of his children. He was awarded £15.

The Peters children are buried in plot E 153, a public grave, in the Nonconformist section.

John Gunsen

John Gunsen, the resident engineer for the Sheffield Water Company, had overseen the construction of the Dale Dyke reservoir and dam. The cause of the collapse was never conclusively identified. The Water Company always denied there were any problems relating to the structure and design of the dam and maintained that the cause of the crack and collapse must have involved a land slip of some kind. The Dale Dyke reservoir was eventually rebuilt in 1875, on a much smaller scale and higher in the Peak District hills. The Water Company continued to support and employ John Gunsen but he was haunted by the disaster for the rest of his life.

He died in 1886 and is buried in the Nonconformist area of the General Cemetery, in plot H 146, under a chest tomb.

Photograph of the Old Dale Dyke reservoir embankment, shortly following its collapse in March 1864. (1864)

Whilst the tragedy of the Great Sheffield Flood provided most of the stories of drowning in Sheffield General Cemetery, there were, of course, other cases of drowning throughout the period. As the next few stories show, the lack of oversight or safety measures, inability to swim and seasonal conditions such as ice, were all factors which contributed to cases of drowning.

Frederick Warburton

Frederick (Fred) Warburton, the son of a Britannia metal smith, was twelve years old when he drowned in Three-square Dam in 1861. At midday he had been sent to Highfields works with his father's dinner. He was told to go straight home, which he did, but then left again to meet his friend Henry Woodhead, who was 13, on Cemetery Road. At

32

Washington Road they were joined by Thomas Thompson, also 12, and the three of them decided to spend the afternoon sliding on the ice on one of the dams below the Cemetery, despite the fact that the ice was thawing fast. Perhaps they thought this was their last chance before the ice went altogether.

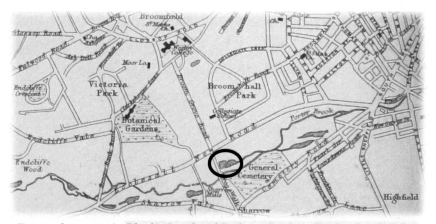

Extract from map in *Black's Road and Railway Guide to England and Wales. Fourteenth edition*, by A & C Black (pub.) (1884) Stalker Mill also known as Three-Square Dams is ringed.

Fred went onto the ice first and eight or nine yards from the side, where the water was nine feet deep, the ice gave way, and he was unable to prevent himself from slipping into the water. Thomas went to help but realising that the ice was bending under his weight, returned to the side. Henry, desperate to save his friend, ran to the edge of the broken ice and tried to pull Fred out but inevitably the ice broke and he also went into the water. All their efforts to climb out were in vain. A workman on the scene, who had previously warned them of the danger, ran to the adjoining wheel to get help. One of the grinders, James Walker, rushed out to see just the boys' hands above the water and although he found a long stick, it was not long enough, and while the other grinders tried to make a rope from several pieces, the boys sank from sight.

The only way to reach the boys was to let the water out, which James Walker did, but this took nearly half an hour. The boys were recovered by a young man employed at the Snuff Mill, the bodies washed and taken to the Nursery Tavern where the inquest was later held. The jury returned a verdict of Accidental Death. Some of the jury expressed the opinion that the dam was dangerous for passers-by because there was no fence.

Although Fred did not have a memorial inscription, there was a quotation beneath the name of Samuel Warburton, another family member, which seems apt in his case too:

> "Stop passenger and read this stone
> and think of how quickly I was gone.
> Death does not always warnings give,
> therefore be careful how you live."

Frederick Warburton is buried in the cleared Anglican area of the Cemetery in the family plot C2 93

Ernest Trevethick

Ernest Trevethick, who was 37 and an insurance agent, was found drowned in the River Derwent at Hathersage. The Sheffield Daily Independent for 6 November 1912 reported that he had been found lying face downwards among some large stones in about 14 inches of water, eight or ten yards from the public footpath which ran alongside. Frost had formed on his back, which had not been immersed; he had clearly lain there all night. He lived in Filey Street with his widowed mother and sister but had left without saying where he was going. His sister said at the inquest that her brother was in the habit of going for a walk in the country to clear his head. He had not seemed depressed, although he had a lot of extra work in connection with his business as insurance agent.

When the body was searched it was found that his pocket watch had stopped at 12.45, and he had a return ticket from Grindleford to Heeley in his pocket. Probably the last person to see him alive was a greengrocer who had spoken to him in Hathersage at 10.45 on the evening of his death. Ernest had asked the way to Grindleford and was told that the last train left at 9.34.

The inquest concluded that Mr Trevethick, having missed the last train to Heeley, had decided to walk to Sheffield. He must have fallen onto stones by the river and drowned while he lay stunned. Why he had chosen to spend the day in Hathersage, and why he had stayed there so late on a winter's evening, remained a mystery. A verdict of 'Accidental death' was returned.

Ernest Trevethick is buried in the Nonconformist part of the cemetery, in plot H 138, which is currently inaccessible. Also, in the same grave are his parents, a brother, and a sister.

Charles Arthur Adams

Charles Arthur Adams died, aged 39, in the wreck of the S.S. Vicksburg off Newfoundland 1st June 1875. The steamer was a British owned ocean liner, built in 1872 in Dumbarton. It made regular sailings between Liverpool, Quebec, and Montreal. On this occasion there was a crew of 60, under Captain Bennet, 7 or 8 saloon passengers and between 20 and 25 steerage passengers. The Rev. C. A. Adams was one of the saloon passengers.

According to a surviving crewman, James Crawley, during the previous evening of 31st May the ship had found itself surrounded by impenetrable ice. The decision was made to head south at a moderate speed, the Captain believing this would enable them to reach less icy seas. Instead, at midnight, the ship struck an ice flow, breaking a propeller and shearing a hole in the iron hull. The crew immediately stuffed whatever they could find into the hole to seal it but by that time a great deal of water was in the hold. They were ordered to throw the cargo overboard to lighten the ship. By 6 a.m. the passengers were becoming anxious- the steerage section was also flooded - but Captain Bennett still felt hopeful that he could bring the ship to safety at St John's, Newfoundland.

Not long afterwards, the report came that water had dowsed the fires in the engine room, and all hope was given up. The order was given to provision and lower the lifeboats. The Captain's lifeboat in which the women passengers had been assigned seats, capsized in the launching. The compass, charts, the rudder, and other essential items were lost. James Crawley, the boatswain's mate, with another crew member who oversaw this lifeboat, began bailing it out, and as they did so three other crew members leapt in. Their boat, with everyone bailing, drifted away from the ship, and they were unable to return.

They saw some people drifting in the sea, clinging to wreckage but were unable to reach them because of the water in the boat and the ice in the sea. Two other boats also got away. The five crewmen drifted for four days before they were picked up by another ship, and taken to New York, all at the point of death from cold and exposure. The Captain and at least 47 of those on board, including Charles Adams, were drowned. Only four passengers reached safety.

The inquiry, held in August, found that the ship had been in good condition and well equipped, but that the company's instructions had not been followed. When ice was detected at 10.30 the previous night, the ship should immediately have hove to until daylight. Instead, the ship kept moving. When the disaster occurred, the crew were ill prepared. They knew which boat they were assigned to, but there had been no practice drills, which explained the difficulties with lowering the boats. The inquiry also noted that the boats should have been lowered earlier, according to the company's written instructions.

Charles Adams had spent part of his childhood in Sheffield Barracks, where his father was a barrack servant. In 1851 Charles, one of four daughters and five sons, was living with his mother, a grocer, in Nether Hallam and working as a clerk to a file manufacturer. Twenty years later he had become an assistant master at a school in Mannington and by the time of his death he was the Reverend Charles

Adams. Sadly, his younger brother James, described as the Reverend James Adams in the burial records, had died six months earlier, two days before their mother also died.

Charles Adam's death is commemorated on plot J1 132 in the cleared Anglican section which contains his mother and brother.

Henry Wharton Shaw and John Shaw

Henry Wharton Shaw was drowned when the inter-island steamer, the SS Penguin, struck rocks and sank off Cape Terawhiti near Wellington harbour, New Zealand.

SS. Penguin (1864)

Women and children were loaded into lifeboats, but these also sank in the stormy seas. Of the 105 people on board, 75 people, including Henry, lost their lives.

Henry, who lived in Melbourne, Australia, had a wife and three children. He was a representative for his father's firm, John Shaw Ltd.,

Yorkshire Wire Works, having been placed in charge of the firm's expanding Colonial trade as a young man. He had gone out to Australia in 1887, and, as reported in the Nelson Evening Mail 15 February 1909, for over more than two decades had largely assisted in the development of their business in Australasia.

Henry died on 12 February 1909. On 17th February his father, John Shaw, despite being in poor health, and accompanied by his wife and daughter, set sail for Australia. He was in Melbourne for about three months, taking care of business, installing Henry's brother Wilfred as the new Australian representative, and presumably doing what he could for his daughter in law and grandchildren. In June, still ill, he embarked on the journey home on the SS Pericles, but his health deteriorated and sadly he died aged 68 before the journey's end. He was buried at sea.

John Shaw had taken control of his father's business, in which he had always worked, in 1868. The wire rope section proved so successful that within a year he had moved to larger premises almost immediately, and even the new premises were enlarged several times. Realising the potential for business abroad, he had travelled several times to South Africa and the Transvaal Goldfields, Natal, Australia, and New Zealand. The Sheffield Daily Telegraph 3 August 1909 reported that: "Although well-known to a large circle of friends and taking a deep interest in all that concerned the welfare of his native town and his fellow citizens, he never cared to figure in public life, preferring that his energies should rather be used in a quiet, unostentatious way than in the turmoil of public life. He was well-known in Masonic circles, being Past Master of the Britannia Lodge in Sheffield, and a Past Provincial Officer of the West Yorkshire Province. He was also one the founders of the White Rose of York Lodge in Sheffield. He will be greatly missed by his brethren in Sheffield and district."

Henry Wharton Shaw and John Shaw are memorialised on the family gravestone for plot W 109 in the Nonconformist area.

George De'Bell (De Bell)

George De'Bell was the son of William James and Eliza De'Bell. William was listed in a Sheffield directory for 1883 as "John De Bell and Son", Moroccan leather manufacturers and hat and cap lining cutters. John De'Bell was the name of William's father who founded the business. George was the second of William's five sons. The eldest son became a teacher, but George went to sea at an early age and on 12 November 1885 at the age of 22, gained his Certificate of Competency as Second Mate. He joined the Polestar, a trading packet built in 1858, as Second Mate, leaving Liverpool probably in late December 1885 on the ship's regular run to South America.

A few months later, on 28 March, heading for Valparaiso, Chile, George De'Bell was swept overboard in a severe gale, 100 miles south of Cape Horn, along with an apprentice. The news did not reach England until the summer. The Mansfield Reporter 2 July 1886 added: "The vessel ultimately reached its destination after what the captain described as 'a long and disastrous passage', the Polestar having been at sea no fewer than 111 days".

George is memorialised along with other members of his family, in plot GG 117 in the Nonconformist area.

TRAGIC CHILDREN

Rufus Roger Hezeltine

Rufus Roger was one of the seven children of Thomas and Alice Hezeltine. Rufus was buried in the family grave, with the inscription: In memory of Rufus Roger, the beloved son of Thomas and Alice Hezeltine who was accidentally killed by a lamb in Sheffield June 11th, 1868, aged 6 years and 8 months.

Sheffield Independent for 13th June reported what happened under the title 'Fatal Accidents':

'Mr W.W. Woodhead held an inquest, yesterday, at the Public Hospital…on the body of a child six years of age, named Rufus Roger Hazeltine, son of Thomas Hazeltine, a spring knife cutler, living in Broad Lane. On Wednesday, the deceased and a number of children were playing in Rockingham Street, when a number of sheep passed by, belonging to Mr Brennan, butcher. One of the sheep got out of the flock, and the deceased and some others ran after it.

Becoming frightened and not knowing where to go, the sheep ran against the deceased, knocking him to the ground. The child's head came into contact with the pavement, and it was subsequently ascertained that the skull was fractured. He was able to walk home, and his mother, not thinking that the injury he had sustained was serious, washed and dressed the wound herself, and did not call in the assistance of a medical man. Death resulted on the following night. A verdict in accordance with these facts was returned.'

Rufus is buried with other family members in plot M3 91, in the cleared Anglican section.

Charles Harris

Nineteenth century newspapers frequently reported the deaths of children from burns. Many of the stories were depressingly similar. Sheffield Telegraph for Monday, 16th March 1874 carried a brief item headlined: "Two Children Burned to Death". On the previous Saturday, Mr Wightman, the Coroner, held two inquests at the Public Hospital. In the first case a little boy was left in a room with a lit fire while the father went upstairs to fetch another child. The first child's clothes ignited when he began playing with the fire. He died next day in hospital. The second case was that of Charles Harris, aged two and a half, who lived with his parents in Cross Turner Street, Suffolk Road. This time it was the mother who lit the fire and then went upstairs to bring down another child. Charles was severely burned, and he too died the following day. The verdict in both cases was "Accidental Death".

Charles Harris is buried in the cleared Anglican area, in plot H4 837, a public grave.

Henry Seyman (Listed as Leyman in burial record)

Henry, known as Harry, was four when he died. Horrifically, he was murdered by his father, Henry on 19th March 1869.

Henry Seyman senior lived with his wife Caroline and five children - Ann, George, Harry, Maria, and William - in Lansdowne Road. He apparently enjoyed reading when he had the opportunity. According to one neighbour's testimony he had always seemed a kind father and fond of his children. Harry was a particular favourite. No motive was identified.

A witness said that Henry senior's mother had died recently, and that Henry had been very depressed as a result. He had also been told by a doctor, treating him for a chest infection, that the nature of his trade - pocket blade grinder - combined with the drinking, would mean he would not be long lived. It was after this that he started drinking much more heavily. The bout seemed to last for two weeks, during which

time he had not worked. When intoxicated, he became violent, terrifying his family.

On the day of the tragedy, Henry senior was in bed at noon, having not returned until 3 a.m. the previous night, very drunk. His wife asked Ann to take him a cup of tea, but she objected. Harry, the four-year-old, did not object, and took the tea. Mrs Seyman waited a few minutes, then went upstairs. There was no sound from the bedroom so she assumed that her husband had taken the little boy into bed with him - as he often did - and had fallen asleep, so she did not look inside the room. A while later, Henry came downstairs, put on his boots, and said, 'Go upstairs and look at Harry. He is dead.' Harry lay on the bed. He had been stabbed violently in the throat with a razor.

Henry Seyman went immediately to the Town Hall to give himself up, but then went away again when he was asked to wait. He returned at 8 in the evening and asked for a 'vagrant ticket' for a place to sleep, which could no longer be obtained there. He was recognised, whereupon he immediately confessed and was arrested. The razor was still in his pocket. He had been drinking. Because he was cold and wet he was allowed to warm himself at the fire.

At the inquest, Henry Seyman "appeared to feel his position most acutely. Whilst the witnesses were being examined, he covered his face with his handkerchief, and at times cried very bitterly. His grief was the most intense when the state in which his murdered child was found was described by two neighbours" (Sheffield Independent 23 March 1869). The jury returned a verdict of Wilful Murder, as directed by the Coroner. Before leaving, Seyman shook hands with two of the witnesses who were neighbours, and 'made some very anxious enquiries of them as to how his wife and children were getting on.'

Sheffield and Rotherham Independent 1st April 1869 also reported on the trial of Henry Seyman at Leeds Assizes Crown Court. Again he 'was much affected and buried his face in his hands during the whole of the time occupied in hearing the case.' Mr Middleton, defending, made the case that the prisoner had been suffering from delirium tremens and had not been responsible for his actions at the time of the murder. After deliberations of half an hour the jury returned with a verdict of 'not guilty, on the ground of temporary insanity.' The judge ruled 'that the prisoner be confined and kept in custody until Her Majesty's pleasure is known respecting what is to be done with him'. Henry Seyman died in 1878 aged 41. Caroline Seyman died in 1903.

Their son is buried in the cleared Anglican in plot K3 43 which was purchased by his mother.

Ruth Sampson

Ruth Sampson, six months old, was murdered by her father, Charles Henry Sampson, a file forger, on 3rd January 1881. The case produced much interest in the local newspapers of the time.

Accounts differ slightly but according to the testimony of family, including Sampson's 11-year-old son and his brother in law, John Owen, aged 28, Charles Sampson had been a good husband and a caring father to his five children. Also living in the family home was his father in law who was in failing health. Mr Sampson had never been a heavy drinker, although some thought he was by no means a steady man. Christmas and New Year was a time for celebration. This Christmas had an additional cause for celebration; Sampson's brother in law, with whom he got on well, was on leave from the 24th Regiment, having just returned from South Africa. Sampson wanted to show him around the town and introduce him to his friends and as a result they drank throughout the Christmas week. John Owen seems to have weathered this regime without injury, but Charles Sampson found he could barely eat while drinking and by December 31st had begun to speak and act very strangely. He was sleeping badly, and when awake, was agitated and restless. So much so that Owen and he visited Mr Thompson, doctor, and surgeon, in Norfolk Street for advice.

According to evidence given at the trial in February, the doctor told Owen to take Sampson home because he was suffering from delirium tremens and might be a danger to himself and others. He was to be given no stimulants of any kind, but when pressed, Mr Thompson relented slightly and said he thought a small glass of port would do no harm. Instead of going straight home, Owen and Sampson went on to two different pubs, where they had a glass of port followed by several pints of beer.

Mrs Sampson also visited Dr Thompson. She said he had advised her to ask for an order to have her husband committed to the Workhouse Asylum, but the next day was Sunday and the parish surgeon, Mr Willington, who could give the order, was at his country residence. Mrs Sampson was unable to see him.

Charles Sampson meanwhile had continued restless and rambling. By evening he was increasingly paranoid and unable to relax. They finally went to bed in the early hours and Owen decided to sleep on the sofa in case he was needed. They had only been in bed for about half an hour when Sampson jumped up and rushed downstairs. Owen persuaded him to lie down on the sofa, but he wanted brandy and Mrs Sampson, thinking that some diluted brandy might help, left to find some. The baby was in the same room as Owen and Sampson. Sampson immediately tried to get up; Owen attempted to hold him down but Sampson, tall and muscular and filled with manic energy, managed to throw him off. Owen was dashed against the dresser and fell to the ground whereupon Sampson knelt on his chest and reached out to the fire grate to grab the poker, swearing to kill his friend. At this point, catching Sampson off balance, Owen managed to throw him off and race out of the house intent on preventing his sister from returning.

Left to himself, Sampson ranged the house, dashing his bare fists through almost every pane of glass in all the windows of the house. At the top of the house he woke his father in law and four older children, smashing the glass there before going downstairs again. His son George, who was eleven, asked if he could come downstairs. Sampson agreed and so it was George who saw the baby lying, not in the basket as he expected, but on the hearth rug. He realised she was dead. His father, dressed only in shirt and trousers, had rushed out and was later found wandering by the police, stiff with cold, his hands and feet lacerated and covered in blood. Believing him insane, they took him to the Workhouse asylum where he confessed to killing his baby daughter. Dr Hunt, the workhouse medical man, examined him and was also of the opinion that he was suffering from delirium tremens. This explained his body going into overdrive, the confusion, the excitement and agitation, and the feelings of paranoia.

The newspapers describe in graphic detail the baby's injuries; she had sustained several fierce blows to the head. Death was instantaneous. The verdict of the inquest was 'Wilful Murder'. Leeds Mercury for 5 February 1881 recorded that at his trial Charles Henry Sampson was found Not Guilty, on grounds of temporary insanity, and was ordered to be detained at Her Majesty's pleasure. The judge added: '…if this will not teach men a lesson of what the consequences of drinking are, I don't know what will.'

Ruth Sampson is buried in plot F 145, a public grave, in the Nonconformist area of the cemetery.

Elizabeth Turner

The death of 13-year-old Elizabeth Turner, perhaps because it was the result of a freak accident in which she was in no way to blame, was reported in detail by the Independent in 1893.

Elizabeth had been asleep on the sofa in the living room of the family home in Radford Street. Near the sofa was a round table on which stood a lighted paraffin lamp. There were several people in the small room, and inevitably someone knocked into the table, which tilted, sending the lamp rolling onto Elizabeth. Her clothes instantly caught fire; the flames intensified by the paraffin which had spilled over her. Only one person, William Wheatley, a forger who 'kept company' with Elizabeth's older sister Eliza, had the presence of mind to try and extinguish the flames by wrapping her in a rug, but without success.

By the time a second rug was found, Elizabeth was unconscious. Most of her clothes had burned away. She was taken to the hospital on a shutter 'wrapped in a couple of overcoats' and died in the early hours. She was the third child and second daughter of Moses, a pocket blade forger, and his wife Ellen Turner.

She is buried in a public grave in the Nonconformist area, plot J 94.

SUDDEN DEATH

Thomas Dawes

George Dawes said at the inquest of eighteen-year-old Thomas that his son was "one of the best lads that ever stepped in shoe leather". Unfortunately, Thomas was also drawn to prize fighting for which he had trained hard over a period. Prize fighting had been popular since the 18th century, but it was illegal, and there were constant reports in the local newspapers of attempts to prosecute the fighters and their enablers. The boxers were always drawn from the poorer classes, tempted by the thought of prize money and a degree of fame, but boxing was brutal and dangerous. Each fight also drew huge unruly crowds.

Sheffield Independent 25th October 1864, reporting on the opening of the Inquest on Thomas Dawes, commented:

"We may state that there is a strong and unanimous feeling on the part of the inhabitants of Pitsmoor that some energetic measures should be taken to stop the shocking practices that are witnessed on every Sabbath day in Old Park Wood…The police do their utmost to prevent these fights, but they know that if they apprehend the ringleaders, and bring them to trial, their punishment will be almost nominal, and they will receive the sympathy of a certain class of persons who uphold what they call the "chivalry" of the prize ring….Last year, a number of prize fighters were prosecuted at the Sheffield Sessions, and they were convicted, with great difficulty, of a breach of the peace…the practical immunity which these men obtain renders them reckless of the law, and is only too well calculated to lead to such brutalising scenes as that which profaned the sanctity of last Sunday."

51

Thomas's parents, who lived in Eldon Street with their nine children, disapproved of their son fighting and Thomas took care to keep them in the dark as much as possible. They did not know of the planned fight. He had not appeared to do any training that week because he had been working. His father knew of the trainer and knew they were friends but did not know the trainer's name. He knew that the trainer had prepared his son for at least one previous contest and brought him home afterwards, but he had not seen him for about two months. Thomas had not come home the night before the fight, which was held at 6.30 in the morning, and the family did not know where he was, until brought the news of his death.

The name of the trainer was William Horner, and, on this occasion, he had acted not as trainer but as combatant. He and Thomas had quarrelled and agreed to fight for '£1 a side.' A witness said that it was an agreed fight, and that Thomas Dawes and William Horner had shaken hands before beginning. William Stenton, known as 'Brick Lad', had been Thomas Dawes' second, and Joseph Potts had acted as Horner's second. The fight had lasted eighteen minutes, with half a minute's rest between rounds. He thought it had been fought fairly. Another witness, Joseph Vardy, knew both men. He lived in the same street as the Dawes family, and he worked in the same factory as William Horner. He had helped to bring Thomas's body home. He thought it was 'a fair stand up fight' and that both had fought well. After the last bout, the deceased had got up when time was called, staggered, and fallen. He died a few minutes later.

The post-mortem examination did not reveal many clues; Thomas Dawes was lean and muscular, the bruises on the body were few and superficial, and the brain appeared healthy, as did the rest of the body. The surgeon, George Kemp, concluded that he had died from 'concussion to the nervous system'.

The jury returned a verdict of "Manslaughter against William Homer (principal), Joseph Potts and William Stent (seconds), and another man unknown to the jury, who acted as umpire and time-keeper."
It is not known what happened to William Horner but William Stent, 'Brick Lad', who acted as Thomas' second, did not change his ways. In 1867 he was meant to be one of the combatants in a fight in Rotherham. The fight did not take place because it was pursued from place to place by the police until eventually the combatants and the huge number of would-be spectators gave up in disgust.

Thomas Dawes is buried in plot L3 157, a public grave, in the cleared Anglican area.

William Hawcroft

William Hawcroft, a widower, was a razor manufacturer who lived in Heeley. He was 67 when he was knocked down by a bullock on Sheffield Moor. The Sheffield Independent 17 December 1868 reported the incident:

"An accident, which does not often take place in the streets of a large town, happened last evening on Sheffield Moor. Mr William Hawcroft, Albert Row, Heeley, was proceeding along the moor, having an umbrella up, when he was attacked by one of two bullocks which were being driven to the slaughterhouse of Mr Gillett. He was knocked down and on a man running to his assistance they were attacked by the second bullock and both of them were pushed to the ground."

Mr Hawcroft had two head wounds one of which was caused by the bullock's horns. The wounds were dressed, and he was sent home in a cab but died two days later.

William Hawcroft is buried in the cleared Anglican section, in plot F1 62 with his wife and other family members.

Advertisement for William Hawcroft Razor Manufacturer, *White's Trade Directory* (1871)

Frederick Grundy

Frederick Grundy was the landlord of the Target Inn beerhouse, Langsett. He had grown up in Lincolnshire and married a local girl, Harriet. They were in Hull in 1861, where Frederick is described as a blacksmith on the census. It is not known what brought them to Sheffield. In his free time Frederick enjoyed repairing guns, and he was a crack shot well known at the Sheffield, Manchester, Liverpool, and other pigeon shooting grounds. It seems particularly ironic that he should have died as he did, aged 40, the victim of a bizarre accident.

Frederick had been playing skittles with three friends and when they tired of skittles, they moved into the taproom of the pub and began a game of dominoes. While they were playing, Fred Grundy fetched a six barrelled revolver and asked if anyone would like to buy it. One man, Charles Naylor, asked for a cap so that he could test it. He had to pull the trigger several times before the cap exploded. Fred Grundy, who had been sitting opposite him, immediately jumped up and cried out "Oh!" before rushing out of the tap room into the kitchen. His friends followed and were horrified to see that blood was pouring from a wound in his throat. Doctors were sent for, but Mr Grundy bled to death within minutes. Charles Naylor, much shocked, went to the Town Hall and reported the incident.

At the inquest, reported in the Sheffield Independent 2nd July 1870, it was established that the men were all good friends. The dying man had managed to tell his wife that Naylor had shot him but did not blame him or say it was intentional. Naylor had asked Fred if there was a charge in the revolver, and Fred had been certain there was not. The revolver belonged to William Unwin, of the Globe Cutlery Works. He was adamant that when he had given it to the dead man it had not been loaded. He said he had previously fired five caps and had tested the sixth which would not fire with a ramrod to see if there was a charge in it and there wasn't. He had asked the dead man to repair the faulty barrel. Mr Grundy was then to sell the weapon for whatever it would fetch. Mrs Grundy, recalled by the Coroner, said her husband would never have loaded the revolver and then told someone it was not loaded.

Although Mr Unwin protested that the pistol was not loaded when he had given it to the deceased, and if there had been any powder left it must surely have fallen out when the barrel was being repaired, the Coroner gave as his opinion that the revolver must have been loaded before it was handed over to Fred Grundy. No blame was attached to Charles Naylor.

The jury returned a verdict of "Homicide by misadventure".

Frederick Grundy is buried in the cleared Anglican area, in the family plot L3 107 with his only child, a son who died three years earlier aged 7, and his wife's niece who died aged 4 in 1864. The inscription for the father reads simply:
"His sun has gone down while it was yet day."

Thomas Ashmore

Thomas Ashmore was by trade a painter, living in Eyre Lane with his wife, when he died following a dog bite. The dog was owned by Mr Davy, landlord of the Exchange Hotel, Egerton Street. The Egerton Hotel was probably well known to Thomas because he had been living there the previous year, and his brother Joseph lived with his family in the same street.

On 10th January 1872, the dog had bitten a small boy who had been teasing it. The child had had to have his finger amputated. In the evening, his father came to tell the landlord. In fact, the landlord had already created a barrier of barrels around the kennel where it was secured. A man named Johnson who heard the conversation, to demonstrate that the dog was friendly, tried to stroke it. The dog immediately bit his hand too. According to one account in the Sheffield Independent, Johnson went to the hospital to have the wound causticed [stet] before returning to the public house. In the meantime, Thomas Ashmore had arrived with some other men and heard the story. Ashmore said they must have teased the animal. He would fetch it and show them – which he did when the landlord, who was not in agreement with this plan, had left the room. The other people present begged him to take the dog out again but instead he patted it on the head. It immediately bit his hand and ran out.

It was shot in Crookes next day, having apparently bitten several dogs, a horse and two children. At first Ashmore was able to work as

usual but gradually he began to show all the symptoms of what was then called hydrophobia and was taken to hospital where he died in dreadful agony.

The Coroner said it was painful to see how little was known about the disease, although it had been recognised for many years. A verdict "That the deceased died from hydrophobia" was returned (Sheffield Independent 14 May 1872). Today the disease is more commonly known as rabies. Until 1885 when a vaccine was developed by Louis Pasteur and Emile Roux, infection resulted in death.

Thomas Ashmore is buried with his mother, brother, and other family members in the cleared Anglican area of the cemetery in plot I2 92.

Robert Fossett

The inscription on Robert Fossett's grave, neatly combining explanation, hope, warning, and a faint threat, reads:

In affectionate remembrance of
Robert Fossett who died May 19th, 1875
.
"Stray mortals here and look upon the stone,
Hoping that I to Heaven have gone.
Death quickly took my sense and strength away
And laid me down upon this bed of clay.
Consider and take home these lines
The grave that is near this may chance be thine."

Robert Fossett was the founder of what became a large and talented circus family, known primarily for their horses, equestrian feats, and clowning. Beginning with trained birds and a 'fortune telling' pony he was able, by the 1860s, to present his own circus. He married his cousin Emma Yelding, an equestrienne, and trained his nine children in circus skills. The eldest, known as 'Sir' Robert Fossett, took the circus very successfully into the 20th century, and his second son, Harry, became well known for his clowning. In 1875, the year of the founder's death at the age of 49, it was a well-reviewed circus, featuring 40 horses and 20 performers, predominantly an equestrian show with 'comicalities from the six great clowns'.

Illustration of Victorian Equestrian Performers by Karen Arnold (publicdomainpictures.net)

According to a family story, Robert died because of a disturbance caused by an unruly section of the audience who pulled one of his daughters from her horse during the performance. The clowns immediately ran back into the ring to defend her, and Robert found the sight so funny and laughed so uproariously that it brought on a fatal seizure. The incident gives an insight into the life of a travelling circus. All the performers, hardened by constant training and life on the road, would be very capable of defending themselves against threat. Robert, amused by the contrast between the clown costumes and the need to fight in earnest, probably felt no need to join in.

His unexpected death meant he was left behind in Sheffield as the touring circus moved on, alone in the grave bought for him, while the Circus continued to entertain in other cities.

Robert Fossett is buried in the cleared Anglican area in plot T2 44.

Joseph Turner

Joseph Turner, a butcher aged 66, was discovered in a field at Lodge Moor on 21st December 1887.

The Sheffield and Rotherham Independent reported that he was in vigorous health and thought nothing of a cross country walk. He had left home at noon on the day of his death, intending to buy 'a beast' from Mr Benjamin Marsden, who farmed just beyond Fulwood. He met Mr Marsden's son in the town and rode with him part of the way, but was dropped off at The Sportsman's Inn, which he did not leave until about 6.45. The landlady was a daughter of Mr Marsden, and she sent a servant to accompany Mr Turner with a lantern. Mr Turner seemed able to take care of himself, so he was left to walk the last part of the journey alone. There was less than a mile to travel and the route was well known to him. This was the last time he was seen alive.

His wife and son assumed he had stayed the night with Mr Marsden and his family, as he had frequently done before, but when he did not return by the evening of the following day, Mr Turner's son Luke began to make enquiries. No one had seen his father. The next morning Luke Turner met Mr Marsden's milk cart in town. Miss Marsden had driven down in it and she told him that his father had not arrived at the farm. Luke Turner, accompanied by a friend, and later by a police constable, began searching all the places his father might have gone. Eventually he was found sitting against a wall, quite dead. He had apparently fallen asleep and then frozen to death.

Joseph Turner is buried in the cleared Anglican section in plot Q2 66 He is one of nine family members in this grave.

Robert Lillyman

Robert Lillyman was killed on 8th July 1888, jumping from a train at Retford. He was a spring knife cutler and had been employed by Messrs Wostenholme and Company for at least five years. He was known as a 'very steady man', and a keen fisherman. Over the years he had frequently travelled to Hayton, near Retford, for a day's fishing. Although the trains which stopped at Retford had been called out at Sheffield Station, tragically he had either misunderstood or misheard and boarded a through train.

One witness, Walter Spiver, from Bolton, was in the same carriage. When the train was almost through Retford station and had not stopped, the deceased said, "For God's sake, what shall I do? I shall have six miles to walk if the train does not stop here." As he went to the door Mr Spiver asked him what he was doing but the deceased pushed him back into his seat and opened the door. Robert Sinclair, also in the same carriage, testified that the deceased had been perfectly sober, but had become anxious when he realised the train was not going to stop, and opened the carriage door. Mr Sinclair tried to stop him, but the deceased had pulled free saying, "Oh my God, I must go," and stepped down onto the footboard. Neither saw what happened next but the travelling inspector in charge of the Manchester, Sheffield and Lincolnshire Railway train and the guard saw a man standing on the footboard. The train had not been booked to stop at Retford and was travelling at between twelve and fifteen miles an hour. They saw the man jump to the ground, but 'his legs shot from underneath him, head twisting to the right, against the train.' He died almost immediately.

The body was identified by John Lillyman, a file forger and Robert's much younger brother. The inquest was held at the Rifleman's Arms, Retford, and reported in the Sheffield Daily Telegraph 11 July 1888. The jury returned a verdict of "Accidental death whilst trying to get out of a train in motion".

Tragically Robert left a wife and three very young children who were left destitute by his death. Unusually, the jury made a present of their fees, 13s, to the widow.

Robert Lillyman is buried in the cleared Anglican area of the Cemetery, in plot Z1 126, with two other family members.

Frederick Charles Hartley

Frederick Charles Hartley was 27 when he died in 1891, and the sole support of his mother. He was an elephant trainer with the well-known and very successful Sanger's Circus. That same year, a review in the Huddersfield Chronicle for 18th October 1892 was hugely appreciative. There were a number of horse riding acts, 'intensely exciting' chariot races, skating displays, high wire artists, comic turns, performing lions and seven elephants which, 'whilst causing a good deal of laughter, were admired for the precision with which they went through their drills.' Three years later the circus was travelling with 160 horses, eleven elephants, a dozen camels and around 330 people. It suggests that Fred was a capable and respected member of the organisation, which would be able to afford the best.

The Sheffield Independent for 31st December 1891 reported "The thousands of people who have witnessed the wonderful performance of the elephants at Sanger's Circus in Sheffield will be shocked to learn that Mr Fred Hartley, the trainer of the animals had died". During the show, the elephants went through a military drill, which ended with the firing of some pistols. Fred always prepared the pistols himself to ensure that they were not overcharged but on Friday 19th December one of the pistols went off accidentally, leaving wadding and powder in the palm of his hand. He went to the Public Hospital for treatment, where it was bandaged and put in a sling, and he was able to carry on as usual. A week later his hand was so painful that he had it dressed again but two days later the hand looked worse and was so much more painful that he was advised to go to the hospital again, where he died a few days later from blood poisoning.

'Sanger's Circus parades through the Wednesday Market in Beverley', East Riding Archives, Ref: DDPD-2-1-32, (1901)

The Independent added that Fred "was extremely well liked by the other members of the circus company". The elephants also seemed to be aware of his loss, for they were said to be unusually restless.

The inscription on his monument read:

"In loving memory of Frederick Charles Hartley, elephant trainer, who died Dec 30th 1891 aged 28 years.

When in my health I little thought the time was come so near
That I should leave all earthly friends that were to me so dear.
Be warned then by my sudden call for death you must prepare,
The time will come you know not where, the manner, how or when."

Fred Hartley is buried in the cleared Anglican area of the Cemetery in plot N2 96.

Thomas W. C. Scrivener (Scribner)

Nothing much is known of Thomas William Charles Scrivener, except what can be gleaned from a report in the Sheffield Independent for 28 December 1893. (The burial records give his name as Thomas William Charles Scribner, while the Death Index and the Independent give his name as Scrivener.) A collier, living in Lansdowne Road, he died for a bet. "A shocking occurrence took place at Sheffield last night as a result of attempting a foolhardy feat. A man named Scrivener, 35 years of age, began boasting of his powers as a beer drinker in the Milton Arms beerhouse, Hill Street and London Road, Sheffield, kept by Mrs Driver, and made a wager with another man named Tomlinson, to drink 12 glasses of beer within the hour. The bet was made, and Scrivener drank nine glasses in half an hour. Immediately afterwards he said, 'I've had enough,' fell back and became unconscious. He was removed to his home in a cab, but a doctor who was called pronounced life to be extinct."

Thomas Scrivener/Scribner is buried in the cleared Anglican
section in plot U2 58, a public grave.

George Sanderson

George Sanderson was one of the nine children of Edmund, a silversmith, and his wife Charlotte. At 14, George, like all his older siblings, was working, in his case as a furniture broker's assistant. Even his younger brother Zachariah, aged 12, was at work as an office boy.

Everything changed six years later in 1897. George, by this time a baker, and still only 20, was in Cemetery Road when he saw a runaway horse pulling a hearse. George did not hesitate but flung himself at the horse's head. The horse was brought to a standstill, but George was killed.

He is buried with his grandparents in the cleared Anglican section, in plot Q2 113

INDUSTRIAL ACCIDENTS

Thomas Chadburn

Thomas Chadburn was a file grinder who worked for Messrs. Wragg and Blackwell, at Mr Marshall's, The Tower Grinding Wheel, in Blonk Street. He was badly injured on the afternoon of Thursday 4th April 1844 when the stone he was using broke. Thomas was thrown several yards from the 'horsing', the saddle like seat from which he worked, onto the 'drum' or wheel, powered by a steam engine, from which belts were attached which drove the grinding stones. He died at home the following Wednesday.

The Sheffield Independent of 13 April 1844 reported on the inquest held at the Ball Lambert Street. Thomas had been conscious and 'did not blame anybody…[he] thought the men above were off work and that the engine consequently went at a greater speed. The engine was lame, and another was put on which always went irregularly.' Thomas Cousins, who had been working next to Thomas Chadburn, agreed that the wheel had been going rather fast but could not say if this had been the case when the stone broke. He did not think the engine was working as regularly as the one it replaced. Despite these reservations, neither man had complained to Mr Marshall.

The report goes on to give a chilling glimpse into the difficulties of the time. Trade Unions were legal from 1825 but during the 1840s, 50s and 60s, some unions used violence against employers and their properties to force change. Workers who did not pay their fees or join the union could also be intimidated. The unrest culminated in the Sheffield Outrages in the 1860s. William Chandler's testimony gives a hint of what was to come. He had not seen the accident but had helped Thomas Cousins to take the injured man home. He reported that a man named John Cocking had that morning wished the stone would break "and knock his brains out", because he, Thomas Chadburn, did not contribute to the Trade's Union. On a later occasion, John Cocking, engaged in "holing a stone", had told Thomas Cousins "Well I've got my wish, and I wish thine may break today, and serve thee the same." Cousins said, "I shall be no worse for that." He said, "I should like to break thy head with this hammer now." Cousins replied, "Thou can't." Cocking said, "But I'll have a knife up to the haft in thee before I've done with thee".

Thomas and his wife had five children listed on the 1841 census, including a ten-year-old son who worked as his father's apprentice. Thomas' widow and the three youngest children are still living together in 1851, his daughters aged 13 and 16 working as scissor burnishers.

Thomas is buried in the Nonconformist area of the Cemetery, in plot V 90, a public grave.

Albert Braddock

Very little is known about Albert Braddock, a joiner aged 31, beyond the account of the fatal accident which was reported in The Sheffield Telegraph 29 November 1894:

"Deceased was a joiner and lived at 70, Walkley Street. On November 5, he was working at some new houses in Fisher Road, Norton, which were being erected by Mr Henry Brown, builder. Whilst working on the roof he fell and sustained injuries which led to his death. Harry Moseley, a joiner, said he was working with the deceased in fixing a dormer light on one of the houses. After deceased had sawn off the log ends of the frame he got up on the top of the house wall to fix the frame. Witness was turning the frame right side up when Braddock called his name. Turning round he saw that he had disappeared, and had fallen to the ground, a distance of 25 feet."

Braddock was at once removed to the Hospital. None of the bricks in the wall had given way. When witness visited him in hospital the following Sunday, Braddock said his foot slipped in the hollow of the spouting. No more scaffolding was required than what was already up. Four feet below the spouting there was scaffolding consisting of two seven-inch battens, supported by "pud locks" fastened to the ordinary scaffolding poles. The width of the top of the wall, together with the spouting, would be about 15 inches, and the spouting would bear the weight of the deceased. Charles Aston, a lad who worked with the deceased, said when he visited Braddock in the Hospital, he told him that his ankle slipped in the spouting, and that caused him to fall. He added that he could not blame anybody for it. Mr Henry Brown, the employer, said the men were working under the usual conditions. The width of the top of the wall, together with the spouting, was 18 inches. *"He had never seen a scaffolding erected especially for the fixing of a roof.* [Editor's italics.]" The jury returned a verdict of 'Accidental death'.

Albert Braddock died 20 days after the accident. He is buried with other family members in the cleared Anglican area in plot L2 61.

David Davy

David Davy was the founder of Davy Brothers, Engineers, Wheelwrights, and Iron Founders.

'Steam Hammer made by Davy Brothers, Sheffield'
photograph by Wendy North (2008)

At the time of his death Davy employed 600 workmen. The Sheffield Independent 14th January 1865 reported:

An "accident of a frightful character occurred yesterday evening at the works of Messrs Davy Brothers, engineers, Blast Lane. It appears that about half-past five o'clock Mr David Davy, senior, was in a part of the works watching the operations of a large Scheil's fan, which has recently been put up, and was used in one of the blast furnaces. Whilst it was revolving with an extraordinary velocity, some portion of it broke off, involving the destruction of the fan, portions of which flew in the direction in which the unfortunate gentleman was standing, and he was struck on the head, and also on the lower part of his body."
Mr Davy was removed, unconscious, to his home in Norfolk Road where he died that evening.

At the inquest, held at the Town Hall, Alfred Davy, his son was "extremely anxious that it should be distinctly understood that there is no blame to be attached to the firm in their mode of working the fan." His testimony, and that of another witness, indicated that the problem might have been a design fault, and in the choice of material for the spindle. However, it was impossible to say exactly what had caused the fan to shatter.

Davy left a wife and six children, the youngest of whom was 14. His nephew, Bernard Walter Davy, Royal Naval Reserve, attached to the Royal Naval Air Service, was killed on active service at Imbros, Gallipoli Peninsula, in 1916. He is buried there and memorialised on the family stone.

David Davy is buried with five other family members in the Nonconformist area of the Cemetery, in plot H 124/5.

ACCIDENTAL OVERDOSE

James Smith

James Smith was one of the sons of William Smith, barrister, and JP, of Dam House. He was a medical student, a pupil of Mr James Ray who was the first person to be buried in the new Anglican section of the Cemetery.

On Sunday 24 June 1850 Mr Smith went to church as usual, then visited a friend, before returning to Mr Ray's house on Glossop Road. Mr Ray had recently died so the house was full of relatives, and Mr Smith had been sharing his room with James Ray's brother, Mr John Ray, for several days. That evening, when Mr Smith asked him if he was ready for bed, Mr Ray replied that he would follow in a few minutes, although in fact it was about twenty minutes later when he went into the bedroom. Normally they chatted for a short time before falling asleep but on this occasion, when Mr Ray went to bed, James' light was out and, as he seemed to be asleep on his side, Mr Ray did not disturb him. Next morning, Mr Ray got up at 6.00 a.m. and spoke to James but when there was no answer, he assumed he was still asleep and left the room. At 8.30, when breakfast was served, there was still no sign of James and a maid was sent to call him. She called, but there was no answer, and she was unable to wake him. Mr Edward Jackson, surgeon, (also buried in the General Cemetery) who lived nearby, was called. He confirmed that James was dead. The body was found with a handkerchief pressed against the nostrils and the head partly covered by bed clothes.

Enquiries established that James had for some days been complaining of pain in his face, including that Sunday, and had been in the habit of inhaling chloroform to alleviate it. He was aware of the danger,

74

because when he had used this remedy in the daytime, he had called Mr Ray's groom into the surgery to sit by him while he inhaled with instructions to rouse him if he remained 'in a stupor' for more than a few minutes. Mr Jackson, giving evidence at the inquest, said that he would not have hesitated to use chloroform in Mr Smith's case. However, although Mr Smith had probably taken his usual amount, "the fact of his lying in a horizontal position when inhaling the chloroform, the head being almost entirely covered by the bedclothes, and his being unable, from insensibility, to remove the handkerchief, would produce the suffocation which resulted in death….I have no doubt that death has resulted from incautiously inhaling chloroform." (Sheffield Independent 29th June 1850) He thought the student had been dead for about five hours.

Tragically, James was still alive when Mr Ray went to bed, because a little later, when composing himself for sleep, Mr Ray heard a groan, and got up on his elbow to listen. When he heard no more, he assumed that James had simply had a bad dream. If he had investigated, perhaps it would not have been too late to rouse him…

James Smith is buried with his father and two brothers in the Anglican area in plot M 16, 17, 36/37.

Henry Morris

Dr Henry Morris, physician, and surgeon had his home at 287 Glossop Road, where he died in 1884 of an accidental chloral overdose at the age of 45. He had bought the practice from Dr Edward Jackson, who, as a young man, had attended James Smith when he died in similar circumstances.

The five-year-old son of Dr and Mrs Morris had died a month before Dr Morris. Following the death, Dr Morris had had great difficulty in sleeping. At the inquest, Dr Mathison, who had been staying with Dr Morris to run the practice, confirmed Mrs Morris' statement that Henry had suffered much since the death of his son, and that it was after this that he began taking chloral to help him sleep. Mrs Morris said he had not seemed well since the death; Dr Matthison thought he had also been driven by grief to drink more than usual during this period.

The jury returned a verdict 'that the deceased died from an overdose of chloral, administered by himself for the purpose of procuring sleep.'

Henry Morris is buried with his son Bertie in the Anglican area plot F 63 and 64, near the main gate on Cemetery Road. Also commemorated was his infant daughter Ella. The gravestone no longer exists.

Map of Sheffield General Cemetery

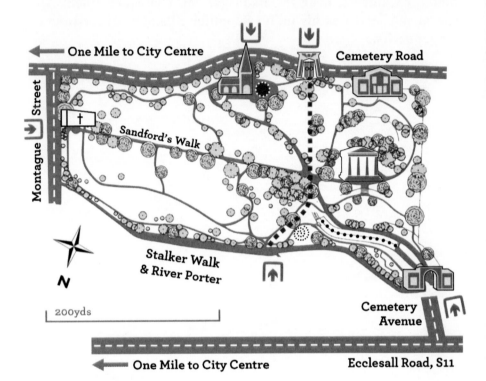

One Mile to City Centre

Cemetery Road

Montague Street

Sandford's Walk

Stalker Walk
& River Porter

N

200yds

One Mile to City Centre

Ecclesall Road, S11

 Nonconformist Chapel
(Samuel Worth Chapel)

 Anglican Chapel

 Egyptian Gate

 Geological Stone Spiral

 Catacombs

War Memorial

Gatehouse

Original Cemetery Office

Dissenters' Wall

Entrance

Alphabetical Index of Featured People

Sheffield General Cemetery Trust

First opened in 1836, the Cemetery was the final resting place for 87,000 people before closing for burials in 1978.

The Cemetery, now a Listed Grade II* Historic Landscape, lay abandoned and overgrown for many years but has been carefully restored by Sheffield City Council and the Sheffield General Cemetery Trust. The many fine buildings, Victorian monuments and headstones now sit in a delightful parkland landscape of wildflowers and shady trees. The Cemetery park is a recognised Local Nature Reserve and its winding paths lead you past some of Sheffield's famous residents, from steel barons to radical chartists.

The Sheffield General Cemetery Trust is a charitable trust which with its committed volunteers maintains and develops the historic landscape and researches the history of the site and people buried there. For over 30 years the Trust has organised events and led tours of the site for the public, schools and community groups. The Trust restored its buildings and the beautiful Samuel Worth Chapel is now available for events hire.

The Cemetery Trust could not exist without its members and volunteers. By joining us as a member for £10 a year you are showing your support for the work we do in maintaining the Cemetery's historic landscape, and in communicating its rich history and wildlife through our events. As a member you will receive regular newsletters, featuring current research on some of the Cemetery's residents, updates on the work we are currently doing and information about what we have planned in the future. Visit our website **www.gencem.org** to find out more about the Cemetery.

"**Murder and Mishap**" is one of a series of books created by volunteers of the Sheffield General Cemetery Trust which can be purchased through our website at **www.gencem.org**

Danger and Despair

A fascinating picture of Victorian life through the vivid descriptions of untimely death. Drawn from the Cemetery's burial records, these are tales of tragic accidents, rejected love, deep despair, and sometimes plain foolishness
Price £7.95 (Paperback) £3.99 (e-book)

Remote and Undisturbed

An illustrated history of the General Cemetery. From its beginnings in 1836 to provide much needed burial space for a rapidly growing city, through to the present day.
Price £7.95

She Lived Unknown

This booklet is a celebration of the lives of women buried in the General Cemetery focusing on poverty, the history of nursing and the way women are symbolised in the Cemetery.
Price £2.95 (Paperback) £1.99 (e-book)

A Life Too Soon Done

Sheffield General Cemetery and the Great War. "A life too soon done" were words inscribed on the family grave of a serviceman killed in the First World War. This book features over one hundred such men from Sheffield who served and died in that War. They are either buried in the General Cemetery or commemorated on family graves there.
Price £7.95